DEFINED

WHO GOD SAYS YOU ARE

A STUDY ON IDENTITY FOR KIDS

YOUNGER KIDS ACTIVITY BOOK
STEPHEN & ALEX KENDRICK
WITH KATHY STRAWN
LIFEWAY PRESS®
NASHVILLE, TN

Published by LifeWay Press® © 2019 Kendrick Bros., LLC
Used under License. All Rights Reserved.

Requests for permission should be addressed in writing to
LifeWay Press®
One LifeWay Plaza
Nashville, TN 37234-0172

ISBN 9781535956765
Item 005814773

Dewey Decimal Classification Number: 268.432
Subject Heading: Discipleship—Curricula\God\Bible—Study
Dewey Decimal Classification Number: 248.82
Subject Heading: CHRISTIAN LIFE \ JESUS CHRIST—TEACHINGS

Printed in the United States of America
LifeWay Kids
LifeWay Resources
One LifeWay Plaza
Nashville, Tennessee 37234-0172

We believe the Bible has God for its author; salvation for its end; and truth,
without any mixture of error, for its matter and that all Scripture is totally true
and trustworthy. To review LifeWay's doctrinal guideline, please visit
lifeway.com/doctrinalguideline.

TABLE OF CONTENTS

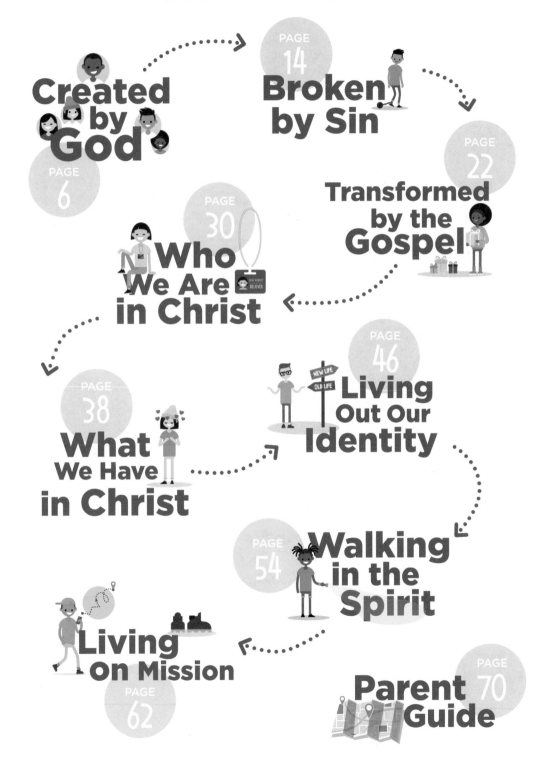

AND YOU WERE **DEAD** IN YOUR TRESPASSES AND **SINS** IN WHICH YOU PREVIOUSLY LIVED ACCORDING TO THE WAYS OF THIS WORLD, ACCORDING TO THE RULER OF THE POWER OF THE AIR, THE SPIRIT NOW WORKING IN THE **DISOBEDIENT**. WE TOO ALL PREVIOUSLY LIVED AMONG THEM IN OUR FLESHLY DESIRES, CARRYING OUT THE INCLINATIONS OF OUR FLESH AND THOUGHTS, AND WE WERE BY NATURE CHILDREN UNDER **WRATH** AS THE OTHERS WERE ALSO.

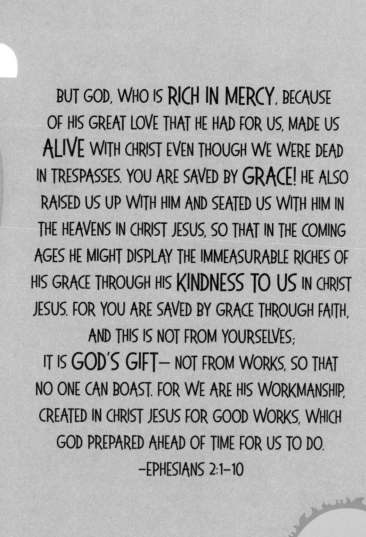

BUT GOD, WHO IS **RICH IN MERCY**, BECAUSE
OF HIS GREAT LOVE THAT HE HAD FOR US, MADE US
ALIVE WITH CHRIST EVEN THOUGH WE WERE DEAD
IN TRESPASSES. YOU ARE SAVED BY **GRACE!** HE ALSO
RAISED US UP WITH HIM AND SEATED US WITH HIM IN
THE HEAVENS IN CHRIST JESUS, SO THAT IN THE COMING
AGES HE MIGHT DISPLAY THE IMMEASURABLE RICHES OF
HIS GRACE THROUGH HIS **KINDNESS TO US** IN CHRIST
JESUS. FOR YOU ARE SAVED BY GRACE THROUGH FAITH,
AND THIS IS NOT FROM YOURSELVES;
IT IS **GOD'S GIFT**— NOT FROM WORKS, SO THAT
NO ONE CAN BOAST. FOR WE ARE HIS WORKMANSHIP,
CREATED IN CHRIST JESUS FOR GOOD WORKS, WHICH
GOD PREPARED AHEAD OF TIME FOR US TO DO.
–EPHESIANS 2:1–10

Created by God

CREATE—
to make, form, and bring into being

Only God is the true Creator.
He can create something from nothing!

KNOW

God created people in His image and for His glory.

UNDERSTAND

God has the authority to determine our identity and purpose.

DISCOVER

The Bible helps us know what being created in God's image means.

KEY VERSE: "FOR WE ARE HIS WORKMANSHIP,
CREATED IN CHRIST JESUS FOR GOOD WORKS,
WHICH GOD PREPARED AHEAD OF TIME FOR US TO DO."
—EPHESIANS 2:10

GOD CREATED PEOPLE

On the sixth day of creation, God created people. He said, "Let's make man in our image. They will rule over the whole earth and take care of all living creatures."

So God made man and woman in His image. God formed the man, Adam, from the dust of the ground. God breathed into him the breath of life. Adam became a living being. God placed Adam in the Garden of Eden where all kinds of trees grew. A river watered the garden. Adam worked the garden and took care of it. God told Adam, "You may eat from any tree in the garden except the tree of the knowledge of good and evil. If you eat from it, you will die."

Then God said, "It is not good for the man to be alone." So God decided to make a helper for the man. God brought all the animals to Adam, and Adam named them. But none of the animals was a good helper for the man. So God put Adam into a deep sleep. He took one of the man's ribs and closed the man's side. God took the rib and made a woman!

God took the woman to Adam. Adam was extremely happy when he saw Eve. "This one, at last," he said, "is bone of my bone and flesh of my flesh."

The woman was a perfect helper for the man; she was his wife.

God blessed Adam and Eve and provided everything they needed.

That was the end of the sixth day. On the seventh day, God stopped and rested because He had completed His work.

–based on Genesis 2

WHO AM I?

Each question has an arrow leading to a piece of the question mark. Read a question, then draw or write your answer in the matching piece of the question mark. Then answer the question in the dot below the question mark.

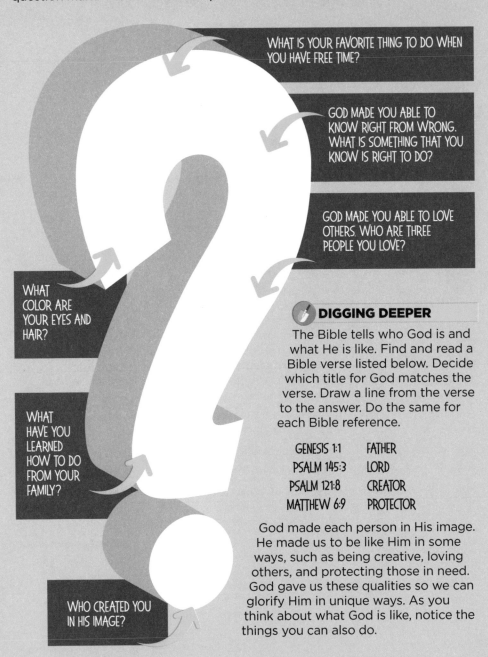

WHAT IS YOUR FAVORITE THING TO DO WHEN YOU HAVE FREE TIME?

GOD MADE YOU ABLE TO KNOW RIGHT FROM WRONG. WHAT IS SOMETHING THAT YOU KNOW IS RIGHT TO DO?

GOD MADE YOU ABLE TO LOVE OTHERS. WHO ARE THREE PEOPLE YOU LOVE?

WHAT COLOR ARE YOUR EYES AND HAIR?

WHAT HAVE YOU LEARNED HOW TO DO FROM YOUR FAMILY?

WHO CREATED YOU IN HIS IMAGE?

DIGGING DEEPER

The Bible tells who God is and what He is like. Find and read a Bible verse listed below. Decide which title for God matches the verse. Draw a line from the verse to the answer. Do the same for each Bible reference.

GENESIS 1:1	FATHER
PSALM 145:3	LORD
PSALM 121:8	CREATOR
MATTHEW 6:9	PROTECTOR

God made each person in His image. He made us to be like Him in some ways, such as being creative, loving others, and protecting those in need. God gave us these qualities so we can glorify Him in unique ways. As you think about what God is like, notice the things you can also do.

JUMP THE HOOPS!

Read Ephesians 2:10. Look for 6 words that stand out to you in the verse. Print each word you choose in a different hoop, starting with the first hoop. Use these words to help you remember the verse. Put a finger on the first hoop. Say the section of the verse with that word. Move to the pink hoop and say that part of the verse. Keep going until you have said the entire verse. Practice until you can say the verse by memory.

If you need to add more words to help you, just draw your own hoops and add the words you need!

DIGGING DAILY

Digging in the Bible means...

➤ reading Bible verses

➤ thinking about what the verses mean

➤ discovering what God wants you to know

At the end of each week's study, you will have a page to use privately as you talk to God in prayer.

Each day will have a Bible passage for you to read and think about. Each day will also have space for you to journal your thoughts, feelings, and questions to God. Now, get digging!

DAY 1

READ GENESIS 1:1, 3, 7, 9, 14, 20, 24

List the things God created in the first six days.

1)

2)

3)

4)

5)

6)

Make a happy face beside the thing you are happiest that God made. Circle the words below that describe God. Mark out any words that do not belong.

CREATOR   POWERFUL   IN CONTROL   LAZY

What are some things you want to talk to God about in prayer?

DAY 2

GENESIS 1:26-28

God created people in His image. This isn't about how you look as much as how you are made inside. God made you to love, to serve others, to be creative, to care for His world, and many other things. What might God want you to do because of the way He made you? Think about your answer and write it below. (You can use a code if you want to keep your answer private.)

....

....

What are some things you want to talk to God about in prayer?

....

....

....

....

DAY 3

READ ACTS 17:24-26

Some people believe God created the world and then left it alone. What do today's Bible verses tell you about whether that is true or not? Look especially at verse 26.

....

....

Verse 26 tells two things God decides about every person. What are they?

1) ....

2) ....

What are some things you want to talk to God about in prayer?

....

....

....

....

DAY 4

READ PSALM 139:13-16

When did God start caring for David, the man who wrote this psalm? (Hint: the answer is in verse 16.)

God has always had a plan for you. He does not force people to follow His plan, but He does have a plan. Unscramble the words below to discover some ways you can know God's plan for you.

EARD ___ THE ELIBB ___

LISTEN TO RETSAHCE ___

LISTEN TO RETSPAN ___

YARP ___

EARLN ___ LEIBB ___ SESVER ___

LISTEN TO THE REAPCHRE ___

What are some things you want to talk to God about in prayer?

DAY 5

READ JEREMIAH 31:3

Forever is a very long time! What does this verse teach you about God's love for you?

Make a list of ways God shows His love to you. Pray, thanking God for loving you forever.

CREATED BY GOD

What is God teaching you about Himself this week? What have you learned about yourself? Is there anything you need to spend time praying to God about?

Use this journal page to write out your prayers and any thoughts you have about what God is teaching you this week. Thank Him for teaching you through His Word.

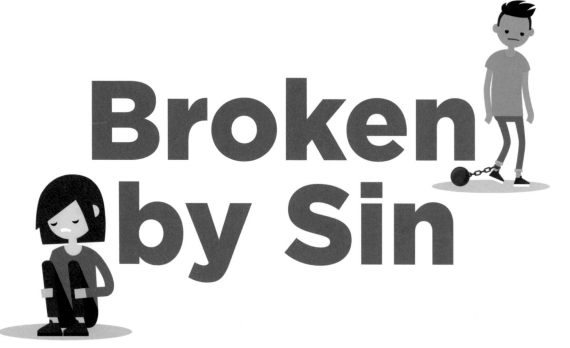

Broken by Sin

BROKEN—
Something that has been torn or fragmented

When people sin, they break the relationship they had with God. They are separated from God by their sin. The good news is that God's plan provides the answer to the brokenness caused by sin.

KNOW
Sin is to think, say, or behave in any way that goes against God and His commands.

UNDERSTAND
All people are broken by sin.

DISCOVER
Before trusting Jesus, our identity is broken by our sin and rebellion against God.

BROKEN BY SIN

ADAM AND EVE SINNED

One day a serpent approached Eve and asked, "Did God really say, 'You can't eat from any tree in the garden?'"

Eve corrected the serpent: "We may eat fruit from any tree except one in the middle of the garden. God said, 'You must not touch or eat that fruit, or you will die.'"

The serpent told Eve, "You won't die! In fact, God knows that when you eat it, you will be like Him, knowing good and evil."

Eve looked at the fruit on the tree. She remembered that the serpent said the fruit would make her wise. Eve took some of the fruit and ate it. She gave some to Adam, and he ate it, too.

Immediately, Adam and Eve realized what they had done. They tried to cover themselves and hide from God.

That evening, God called out to Adam. "Where are you? Did you eat from the tree I commanded you not to?"

Eve said, "The serpent tricked me, and I ate it."

God told the serpent, "Because you have done this, you are cursed more than any other animal. You will move on your belly and eat dust." Then God told Eve, "You will have pain when you have a baby." God told Adam, "You must work hard to grow your food now, and one day you will die."

God made Adam and Eve leave the garden.

— based on Genesis 3

KNOCK! KNOCK!

To find the answer to the question on each door, gather all the words with the same number from the keys. Write them in the door with their number on it. Rearrange the words to get the answer to the question.

Read Ephesians 2:1. Remember that when people sin, they are separated from God. Cross out the fingerprints that don't match the original in order to find out who sins.

ORIGINAL

B A R L S M T F L

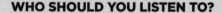

WHO SHOULD YOU LISTEN TO?

Satan wants people to disobey God. Look at the thought bubbles. Print a *T* in the bubbles with words Satan might tempt you to act on. Print a *O* in the bubbles with thoughts God wants you to obey. Satan will tempt you to do wrong things. God sent the Holy Spirit to help you overcome temptations.

DIGGING DAILY

Digging in the Bible means...

➤ reading Bible verses,

➤ thinking about what the verses mean,

➤ discovering what God wants you to know.

At the end of each week's study, you will have a page to use privately as you talk to God in prayer.

Each day will have a Bible passage for you to read and think about. Each day will also have space for you to journal your thoughts, feelings, and questions to God. Now, get digging!

READ EPHESIANS 2:1 AND GENESIS 3:1-3

What was different about what Satan said and what Eve said about what God commanded?

Look at Genesis 2:16. Who was right? Circle your answer.

SATAN   EVE   BOTH OF THEM   NEITHER OF THEM

What do you want to talk to God about today?

READ EPHESIANS 2:2 AND GENESIS 3:4-6

Satan always lies. He wants you to disobey God. How did Satan lie to Eve? Why was Eve tempted by Satan's lie?

The Bible does not tell what kind of tree was in the garden, but Eve saw three things about it. List them here.

1)

2)

3)

Eve spent time thinking about the tree. That made it easier for Satan to tempt her to eat it. God wants you to think on His words, not Satan's.

What are some things you want to talk to God about in prayer?

DAY 3

READ EPHESIANS 2:3 AND GENESIS 3:6-8

What wrong things did Eve do AFTER she ate the fruit? Make a check mark beside the wrong things Eve did.

- ☐ GAVE FRUIT TO ADAM
- ☐ HID FROM GOD
- ☐ THANKED SATAN
- ☐ SOLD THE TREE

Disobeying God is sin. Sin has consequences. What kind of consequences have you seen someone suffer because they did something wrong?

What are some things you want to talk to God about in prayer?

DAY 4

READ EPHESIANS 2:10 AND GENESIS 3:8-11

Adam and Eve suffered consequences to their sin right away. Did you notice that they hid from God instead of talking with Him as they had done before? Did you notice that they were afraid and that they realized they were not clothed? Sin separated Adam and Eve from God and changed their relationship with Him.

Think about a time you have done something wrong. What happened because of what you did? (You can write in code if you want to keep this private.)

What are some things you want to talk to God about in prayer?

DAY 5

READ EPHESIANS 2:11 AND GENESIS 3:12-13

Who did Adam blame for his sin?

Who did Eve blame?

When someone is caught doing something wrong, he often blames someone else. For example, if two kids are fighting and a teacher stops them, each of them might say that the other one started it!

How do you think God feels when people blame others instead of telling the truth about what they have done?

What is God teaching you about Himself this week? What have you learned about yourself? Is there anything you need to spend time praying to God about?

Use this journal page to write out your prayers and any thoughts you have about what God is teaching you this week. Thank Him for teaching you through His Word.

BROKEN BY SIN

Transformed by the Gospel

TRANSFORMED—
changed completely

When a person trusts Jesus as Savior, he is changed completely. He is forgiven of sins, adopted into God's family, wants to act differently, and is full of God's love.

KNOW

Trusting in Jesus for salvation transforms your identity.

UNDERSTAND

God's salvation is eternal. Nothing can separate believers from God's love.

DISCOVER

God's salvation is a gift that every person needs and can receive.

SAUL'S CONVERSION

Saul was an enemy of those who believed in Jesus. Saul entered house after house and dragged the believers away to prison. He made murderous threats against Jesus' followers, requesting permission from the high priest to travel to Damascus and arrest believers there.

As Saul was near Damascus, a bright light from heaven flashed around him. The light blinded Saul, and he fell to the ground. He heard a voice ask: "Why are you persecuting (hurting) Me?" "Who are You, Lord?" Saul asked.

"I am Jesus, the One you are persecuting," was the answer. "Go into the city. You will be told what to do."

Saul's traveling partners led him to the city. He could not see for three days. God told a man named Ananias, "Go to Saul. He has been praying. He knows you are coming to help him see again."

Ananias replied, "Lord, I have heard how much evil this man has done." God replied, "Go because I have chosen this man to tell the Gentiles about Me!" Ananias obeyed. When he put his hands on Saul's eyes, Saul could see again. Saul was baptized and immediately began to preach in the synagogues about Jesus. "Jesus is God's Son!" Saul announced.

Some Jews were angry with Saul's new message. They plotted to kill him. Saul's friends helped him escape Damascus by lowering him over the wall in a basket. Saul went back to Jerusalem and continued to speak boldly about his faith in Jesus.

—based on Acts 9:1-20

TRANSFORMED BY THE GOSPEL

TANGLED WEB

Read the questions and try to answer them. Then follow the path from a question to the answer to find out if you are right.

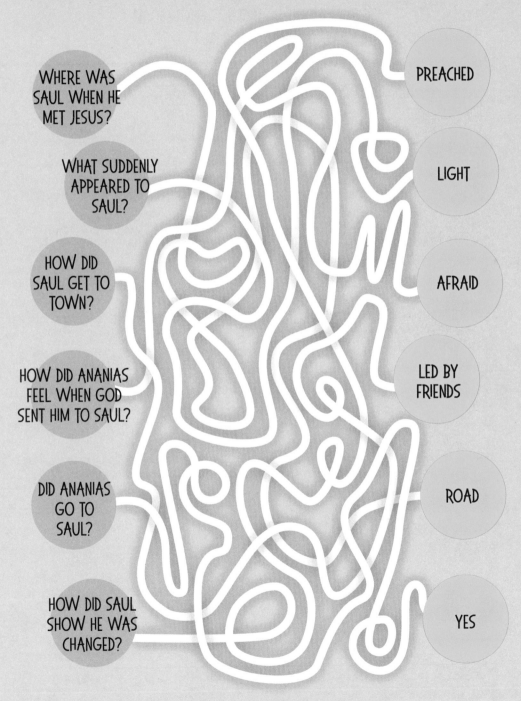

WHERE WAS SAUL WHEN HE MET JESUS?

WHAT SUDDENLY APPEARED TO SAUL?

HOW DID SAUL GET TO TOWN?

HOW DID ANANIAS FEEL WHEN GOD SENT HIM TO SAUL?

DID ANANIAS GO TO SAUL?

HOW DID SAUL SHOW HE WAS CHANGED?

PREACHED

LIGHT

AFRAID

LED BY FRIENDS

ROAD

YES

IT'S A GIFT!

Close your eyes and try to touch a gift on this page with your index finger. Open your eyes and see how you did. Tell whether the word printed on the gift is true about God's gift of salvation. Take turns with a friend or play by yourself.

GIVEN GLADLY
BROKEN
NO CHARGE
FREE
GENEROUS
CAN BE TAKEN AWAY
SOMETHING GIVEN

EPHESIANS 2:8-9 SAYS THAT GOD FREELY AND GLADLY GIVES THE GIFT OF HIS GRACE FOR SALVATION TO THOSE WHO TRUST JESUS AS SAVIOR AND LORD.

DIGGING DEEPER

In Acts 9, Saul was changed completely when he met Jesus and trusted Him as Savior. In Ephesians, Paul told more about people being changed by trusting Jesus. Read Ephesians 2:1-5. Then choose the correct word to fill in each blank to explain what Paul wrote. (words to use: God, Everyone, saved, Sin, loved)

_____ SEPARATES PEOPLE FROM GOD.

_____ SINS AGAINST GOD SOMETIME IN THEIR LIVES.

WE ARE _____ SO MUCH BY

_____ THAT HE MAKES US ALIVE IN CHRIST.

PEOPLE ARE _____ BY GRACE.

DIGGING DAILY

Digging in the Bible means...

➤ reading Bible verses,

➤ thinking about what the verses mean,

➤ discovering what God wants you to know.

At the end of each week's study, you will have a page to use privately as you talk to God in prayer.

Each day will have a Bible passage for you to read and think about. Each day will also have space for you to journal your thoughts, feelings, and questions to God. Now, get digging!

READ ACTS 9:1-2

What did Saul intend to do? Do you think Saul loved Jesus in these verses? Why or why not?

Read 1 John 4:19. Did God love Saul?

God has always loved you. What are some ways you can tell that God loves you? (Hint: You can start with ways He takes care of you.)

Write a prayer here thanking God for what He has done for you.

READ ACTS 9:3-9

How might you feel if you suddenly saw a blinding light and heard a loud voice? How do you think Saul felt?

What was different about Saul when the light went away? Circle the right answer.

HE WAS SUDDENLY IN A DIFFERENT CITY.
HE WAS BLIND.
HIS FRIENDS WERE GONE.

Who did Saul hear speaking? [ ] [ ] [ ] [ ] [ ]

Today we know more about Jesus by reading the Bible and by praying. What are some things you want to pray about today? Note those things here, then spend time talking to God and listening to Him.

....

....

....

READ ACTS 9:10-13

God wanted Ananias to visit Saul and heal him. Starting with the second letter, cross out every other letter on the line below to find out how Ananias might have felt.

S X C L A I R V E K D

Have you ever needed to do something that was scary to you? Maybe you had to talk to the whole class, face a bully, or stay home alone for a short time. The good news is that God promises to be with us no matter what we face.

List any things that scare or bother you. Then talk to God about helping you.

....

....

....

....

....

DAY 4

READ ACTS 9:17-20

How do you know that Saul was completely changed after trusting Jesus? What might change at school for a kid who trusts in Jesus? At home? At practice?

Saul preached about Jesus in the synagogues. Most kids don't get to preach anywhere. How else might a kid tell about Jesus?

Talk to God about places and people you can tell about Jesus.

DAY 5

READ EPHESIANS 2:8-9

Who loves you as much as God loves you? Your mom? Your grandfather? Your best friend? Those people love you so much, but God loves you even more. No one loves you as much as God loves you.

Even though people sinned and broke God's perfect plan, God loved people so much that He sent Jesus to take the punishment for their sin. Jesus paid the price for our sin so we would no longer be separated from God. However, each person must receive God's gift of salvation. You can receive this gift when you admits to God that you are a sinner and are sorry for your sin, wanting to turn away from sin. You must believe that Jesus is God's Son and that Jesus is the only way to be saved from sin. (You can't do it yourself!) Then you tell others that your trust is only in Jesus and what He did for you by His life, death, and resurrection.

Talk to God today about which of these things you have done, want to do, or are just thinking about.

What is God teaching you about Himself this week? What have you learned about yourself? Is there anything you need to spend time praying to God about?

Use this journal page to write out your prayers and any thoughts you have about what God is teaching you this week. Thank Him for teaching you through His Word.

Who We Are in Christ

ADOPTED—
taken or chosen as one's own

When a person trusts in Jesus as Savior, God brings that person into His family as His own son or daughter.

KNOW
You are who God says you are

UNDERSTAND
Everyone who trusts in Jesus receives a new identity.

DISCOVER
God defines the true identity of all followers of Jesus.

KEY VERSE: "BUT GOD, WHO IS RICH IN MERCY, BECAUSE OF HIS
GREAT LOVE THAT HE HAD FOR US, MADE US ALIVE WITH CHRIST
EVEN THOUGH WE WERE DEAD IN TRESPASSES.
YOU ARE SAVED BY GRACE!"
—EPHESIANS 2:4–5

THE VINE AND THE BRANCHES

Jesus said, "I am the true vine. My Father is the gardener. The gardener cuts off every branch in Me that does not produce fruit. However, if a branch is producing fruit, He prunes it (cuts off just the dead parts) so the branch can continue to produce fruit."

Then Jesus reminded His disciples they are already followers of Him. Jesus told His disciples He wanted them to remain in Him, just like a healthy branch produces fruit when it stays attached to the vine. He explained that He would remain in them, too. He pointed out that a branch broken off the vine cannot produce any fruit but must stay connected to the vine in order to produce fruit.

Again, Jesus repeated, "I am the vine" This time, however, He added that His followers were the branches. He urged them to remain in Him in order to produce much fruit. He said, "Without Me, you can do nothing. If you don't remain in Me, you are like one of the branches that is carried off to be burned up."

Jesus encouraged the believers to remain in Him and in His words. "God is glorified when you produce much fruit and show that you are My disciples," Jesus said.

— based on John 15:1-8

WHO WE ARE IN CHRIST

COUNT, WRITE, READ!

Count how many letters are in each of these words from the Bible study.

BELIEVER: ☐ BRANCH: ☐

JESUS: ☐ REMAINS: ☐

How were the words important in the story?

Write each word in the right place on the grid. Write the shaded letters in order from bottom to top.

Read the word you discovered. How was this word important in today's Bible study?

DIGGING DEEPER

Read Ephesians 2:4-5. Below are three words from the verses and three definitions. Draw a path from each scooter to its definition.

GRACE

FAITH

MERCY

NOT RECEIVING PUNISHMENT YOU DESERVE

TRUST OR BELIEF

RECEIVING WHAT YOU DO NOT DESERVE

WHAT'S IT SAY?

Match each clue to a robot, then write the clue word on the robot it matches.

CLUES

🔍 BELIEVERS   🎧 WANTS   ✴ ARE ADOPTED

INTO GOD'S   🎮 BELIEVERS   🥕 ARE FORGIVEN

🎓 WHAT GOD   🛹 SINS.   🍔 BELIEVERS

⭕ BEGIN WANTING   👓 OF THEIR   💗 FAMILY.

What does this tell about believers in Jesus?

FAMILY.

What does this tell about believers in Jesus?

What else do you learn about believers in Jesus?

DIGGING DAILY

Digging in the Bible means...
- ➤ reading Bible verses,
- ➤ thinking about what the verses mean,
- ➤ discovering what God wants you to know.

At the end of each week's study, you will have a page to use privately as you talk to God in prayer.

Each day will have a Bible passage for you to read and think about. Each day will also have space for you to journal your thoughts, feelings, and questions to God. Now, get digging!

READ JOHN 15:1

Who is the vine? ....

Who is the gardener? ....

Jesus gave His followers a word picture to help them understand Him and His Father better. A gardener does what is best for his plants. God loves Jesus more than a gardener loves plants.

Draw a plant. Beside the plant, draw a gardener. (Stick figures are OK.) Label the plant as Jesus and the gardener as God.

Praise God in your prayer today for loving you so much. ....

....

....

....

DAY 2

READ JOHN 15:2

What does a gardener do with branches without leaves? He cuts them off to keep the vine healthy. When God knows believers are choosing wrong things, He helps them see what needs to change. He helps them change if they ask Him. Talk to God today about what might need to change in your life to keep you connected to Jesus. You might need to start doing something or you might need to stop doing something. God will help you know what to do if you ask Him.

DAY 3

READ JOHN 15:3-4

In verse 4, what did Jesus tell His disciples to do?

Fill in the vowels to help you recall some words that mean the same as remain in.

You are doing something right now that will help you remain in Jesus—Bible study and prayer!

Talk to God and tell Him what is easy about being united with Him and what you find hard to do. Write your prayer here.

DAY 4

READ JOHN 15:5.

Who does Jesus say He is? ....

....

Jesus is the vine, and believers in Him are the branches of the vine.
Jesus is not telling people to grow bananas or grapes. Jesus meant that His believers should tell others about Him so they can be believers, too.

What does Jesus say people can do if they do NOT remain in Him? Find the answer in verse 5.

☐ ☐ ☐ ☐ ☐ ☐

Ask God to help you notice times you can tell others about Him. Ask Him to help you know what to say. ....

....

DAY 5

READ EPHESIANS 2:4-5

Write down four or five words from the verse that make you think about what God is like. ....

....

Circle the one you like best. Why did you pick that one?

Being alive in Christ means a person has changed from being separated from God. You can't make that change in yourself. It has to come from God.

What would you like to talk to Jesus about today? You can write it here or just think it. ....

....

What is God teaching you about Himself this week? What have you learned about yourself? Is there anything you need to spend time praying to God about?

Use this journal page to write out your prayers and any thoughts you have about what God is teaching you this week. Thank Him for teaching you through His Word.

WHO WE ARE IN CHRIST

What We Have in Christ

LOST—
describes people without God

Although all people sin, not all people trust Jesus to save them from the punishment of their sin. Those who have not believed that Jesus is the only way to be a child of God are described as lost. People who have trusted Jesus are described as saved.

KNOW
When we trust in Jesus, God adopts us and welcomes us into His family as His children.

UNDERSTAND
Jesus came to seek and to save the lost.

DISCOVER
We receive the blessing of eternal life as an inheritance from God.

JESUS TAUGHT THREE PARABLES

Tax collectors and sinners came to listen to Jesus teach. The religious leaders complained because Jesus welcomed sinners, so Jesus told them three parables to teach them about God.

Jesus said, "If a man has 100 sheep and loses one, what does he do? He leaves the 99 sheep in the open field and searches for the lost sheep until he finds it. Then he tells his friends, 'Let's celebrate! I found my lost sheep!'" Then Jesus said, "This is what heaven is like; there is more joy in heaven when one sinner repents and turns back to God than for 99 people who did not wander off."

Jesus said, "If a woman has 10 silver coins and loses one of them, what does she do? She lights a lamp, sweeps the house, and searches carefully until she finds it! Then she tells her friends, 'Let's celebrate! I found my lost coin!' " Then Jesus said, "This is what heaven is like. There is joy in heaven when one sinner repents and turns back to God."

Finally, Jesus said, "A man had two sons. The younger son said, 'Father, give me my inheritance today.' So the father gave his son his share. The younger son left home. He wasted his money and lived foolishly. There was a famine, and the people there did not have enough food. The son got a job feeding pigs. He was so hungry, even the pigs' food looked tasty."

"The younger son made a plan. He would go back to his father and admit he was wrong. He would ask to work for his father like the servants."

"So the younger son headed home. He was still a long way away when his father saw him coming. His father ran to him, threw his arms around him, and kissed him. The son began to apologize. 'I have sinned against God and against you,' he said."

"But the father told his servants, 'Let's celebrate with a feast! Bring the best robe and put it on my son! Put a ring on his finger and sandals on his feet. This son of mine was lost, and now he is found!'"

"At this time, the older son came from the fields and heard music at the house. 'What's going on?' he asked one of the servants."

"'Your brother is here,' the servant said. 'Your father is celebrating.' "The older brother was angry! He refused to go to the feast. The father asked him to come inside. 'Look!' the older brother said. 'I never disobeyed you! But you never threw a party for me.'"

"'Son,' the father said, 'everything I have is yours. We have to celebrate and be happy. Your brother was lost and is found.'"

— based on Luke 15

PLAY BALL!

Look at the baseballs below. Cross out each one that does not look like this:

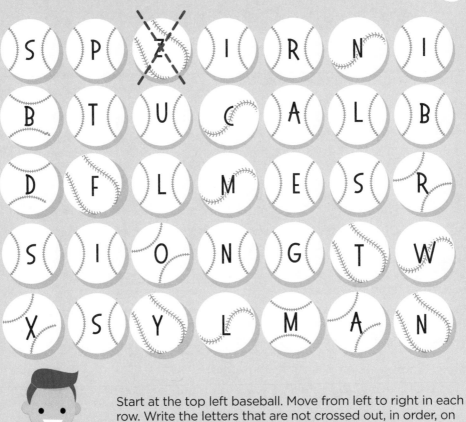

Start at the top left baseball. Move from left to right in each row. Write the letters that are not crossed out, in order, on the blanks below. What do believers have in Jesus?

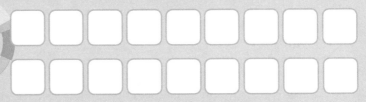

You can check Ephesians 1:3 to see if you are right!

X'S AND O'S

Circle the pictures that show what was lost in the stories Jesus told in Luke 15. Cross out the other pictures.

🔍 DIGGING DEEPER

Jesus told three stories in Luke 15. Fill in the chart below after you find and read the verses. Write who lost something, what was lost, and how the finder felt.

	WHO?	WHAT?	HOW?
LUKE 15:4–6			
LUKE 15:8–9			
LUKE 15:11,13, 20,22–24			

Jesus told these three stories to help people know He came to find and to save those who are lost. Remember, the word *lost* describes people without God. Jesus wants lost people to come to God, so He finds them and calls them to trust in Him as their Savior and Lord.

DIGGING DAILY

Digging in the Bible means...

➤ reading Bible verses,

➤ thinking about what the verses mean,

➤ discovering what God wants you to know.

At the end of each week's study, you will have a page to use privately as you talk to God in prayer.

Each day will have a Bible passage for you to read and think about. Each day will also have space for you to journal your thoughts, feelings, and questions to God. Now, get digging!

READ LUKE 15:3-7

Who told this story?

Have you ever lost something? How did you feel? Sheep were important to their owners in Bible times. They used their wool for clothing and blankets. They used them for food. When the sheep was found, everyone rejoiced with the owner. Did you find what you lost? How did you feel then? God feels even more joy when someone trusts Him.

Thank God today for loving you so much.

READ LUKE 15:8-10

Jesus told this story of a woman losing a costly coin. She had to search the whole house looking for it. Did she find it?

☐ YES ☐ NO

How did she feel then?

Jesus said there is happiness in heaven when any sinner repents from sin. People are valuable to Jesus. He wants each of them to trust Him and come to God.

Spend time today thanking Jesus for always seeking to bring lost people to God.

....

....

....

....

DAY 3

READ LUKE 15:11-19

The younger son left home and spent all his money foolishly. What made him decide to go back home to his father?...

....

....

The young man decided to ask to be a servant in his father's house. How might it be different to go back home as a servant?...

....

....

....

....

One of the spiritual blessings God gives to believers is adoption into His family as His children. Thank God today that He loves everyone and wants them in His family...

....

....

....

....

READ LUKE 15:20-24

How did the father welcome his son back home? ....

....

....

The father had not misplaced his son, but he didn't know where he had gone. The father was happy to see the son. What in the Bible verses helps you know he was happy? ....

....

....

Jesus told three stories about lost things that were found. He wanted people to know that He came to seek those who were without God and to save them from their sins.

What are some things you want to talk to God about in prayer? ....

....

....

READ EPHESIANS 1:3-7

Paul was thankful to God when he wrote these verses. He thought about all the blessings God had given him.

Find these words (or words that mean the same thing) in the verses. Check off each one as you find it.

☐ ADOPTED ☐ REDEMPTION ☐ FORGIVENESS ☐ WISDOM

If you have already trusted Jesus as Savior and Lord, thank Him for these blessings and others He gives.

If you have not yet trusted Jesus as Savior and Lord, thank Him for preparing blessings for you when you do make that decision. ....

....

....

What is God teaching you about Himself this week? What have you learned about yourself? Is there anything you need to spend time praying to God about?

Use this journal page to write out your prayers and any thoughts you have about what God is teaching you this week. Thank Him for teaching you through His Word.

WHAT WE HAVE IN CHRIST

Living Out Our Identity

IDENTITY IN CHRIST—
Who God says you are

When a person becomes a Christian, her identity is changed.
The person looks the same on the outside, but she is a
different person in the ways she thinks,
feels, and acts.

KNOW

We are responsible
for our choices.

UNDERSTAND

Repentance is
turning away from
sin and turning to
Jesus.

DISCOVER

As disciples we
grow in our faith
and knowledge of
Jesus.

PETER DENIED JESUS AND WAS FORGIVEN

On the night before Jesus was crucified, Peter shared the Passover supper with Jesus and the other disciples. Jesus said, "Peter, Satan will test you, but I have prayed that your faith will not fail." Jesus encouraged Peter to come back to the disciples afterward and to help them be faithful.

Peter said, "Lord, I am ready to go with you to prison or to die."

Jesus said, "Before the rooster crows today, you will deny three times that you even know Me."

Later that night, Jesus was arrested. Peter followed and waited outside. A servant girl said, "This man was with Jesus." Peter quickly said, "I don't know Him!" Someone else said, "You're one of His followers!" Peter said, "No, I am not!"

A third person said, "He is from Galilee. He was with Jesus." Peter said, "I don't know what you are talking about!" Just then, the rooster crowed. Jesus turned and looked at Peter. Peter ran away, crying over what he had done.

But the story isn't over! After Jesus' resurrection, Peter and other disciples were fishing. They had not caught any fish all night long. At sunrise, Jesus stood on the shore, but the disciples didn't recognize Him. Jesus told the men to throw their net on the other side of the boat to find fish. As soon as they did, the net was full of fish!

One of the disciples said, "It is the Lord!" Peter jumped into the water and hurried ashore before the others. The men ate breakfast on the shore with Jesus.

Three times, Jesus asked Peter, "Do you love me?" Three times, Peter answered, "Yes. You know I do!" Three times Jesus told Peter to feed His sheep, meaning for Peter to take care of Jesus' followers.

Three times Peter had denied knowing Jesus and now three times Jesus asked if Peter loved Him. Three times Jesus told Peter there was still work for him to do.

Later, Peter was with the other disciples in Jerusalem when the Holy Spirit came on them and they spoke in many languages. When people wondered what was happening, Peter preached to the crowd. He told them about Jesus He begged the listeners to believe in Jesus as Savior. About 3000 people became believers that day!

Years later, when Paul wrote a letter to the Colossians, he urged believers to live lives that were true to what Jesus and the Scripture taught. Paul challenged the people to be compassionate, kind, humble, gentle, and patient. "Do everything in the name of Jesus," Paul wrote.

–based on Luke 22:31-34; 54-62; John 21:1-19; Acts 2, Colossians 3

LIVING OUT OUR IDENTITY

DISCOVER THE BUBBLE

Use the bubbles to help you discover another word that means to turn from sin and turn to Jesus. Read the clues and write the correct letter in the bubble. Then write the letters in order below.

WHEN A PERSON ADMITS HIS SIN TO GOD AND TURNS AWAY FROM THE SIN,

HE ◯ ◯ ◯ ◯ ◯ ◯

I am in PATH and POSE.

I am in HOME and RED.

I am in NEST but not BEST.

I am in PEACE and LOVE.

I am in TOP but not POP.

I am in ROW but not TOW.

I am in YES and SAT.

NUMBER MATCH

Match each question with the correct answer.

HOW MANY TIMES DID JESUS ASK PETER A QUESTION?

HOW MANY TIMES DID PETER ANSWER JESUS?

HOW MANY TIMES DID JESUS TELL PETER HE HAD WORK TO DO?

HOW MANY TIMES DID PETER DENY KNOWING JESUS?

III

THREE

3

What do the answers to these questions make you think?

DIGGING DEEPER

Read Ephesians 4:25. What does the verse tell is a wrong way to act? What right way is mentioned?

Read Ephesians 4:29. Which action is right and which one is wrong?

Read Ephesians 4:32. What actions are listed here?

Becoming a Christian does not mean that a person never sins again. Christians still sin because we have hearts that want to sin, but we can say no to sin by asking God for help. When Jesus returns, He will make us sinless like Him.

LIVING OUT OUR IDENTITY

DIGGING DAILY

Digging in the Bible means...
- ➤ reading Bible verses,
- ➤ thinking about what the verses mean,
- ➤ discovering what God wants you to know.

At the end of each week's study, you will have a page to use privately as you talk to God in prayer.

Each day will have a Bible passage for you to read and think about. Each day will also have space for you to journal your thoughts, feelings, and questions to God. Now, get digging!

DAY 1

READ LUKE 22:31-34

Simon is another of Peter's names. What did Peter promise to do for Jesus? Jesus warned Peter that he would tell others he didn't know Jesus. Not one time, but three times!

Peter wanted to do what was right. What are some things you want to do that are right but might be hard?

No one always makes right choices. One good plan is to ask God to help you make right choices.

When you pray today, ask God for help with anything you have trouble doing. He is always ready to hear and to help.

DAY 2

READ LUKE 22:54-57

The very same night that Peter promised to go with Jesus even if he went to prison, Jesus was arrested. Peter waited outside. Who asked Peter if he knew Jesus according to verse 56?

Did Peter tell the truth? ☐ YES ☐ NO

Why might Peter have lied to the servant?

When might be a time that kids today would be afraid to tell someone about Jesus?

Jesus knows people are sometimes afraid, but He has promised to be with them. Talk to God today and ask who He wants you to tell about Him.

READ JOHN 21:15-17

The story in these verses happened after Jesus had risen from the dead. His disciples had seen Him a few times. Now the disciples were on the shore of the lake. They had breakfast with Jesus. Then Jesus asked Peter a question.

What would you say if someone asked you if you loved Jesus?

Peter did love Jesus even though he felt terrible about denying Him. Jesus gave Peter work to do. He was to take care of Jesus' followers.

God has a plan for you too! You might not know all the plan yet, but you do know Bible verses about how God wants you to act. What are some things you know God wants you to do?

Thank God today that He has a plan for you.

DAY 4

READ LUKE ACTS 2:1-4

What happened after the wind from heaven came? ....

....

Peter was one of the disciples in the room when the Holy Spirit came to them. Everyone began to preach in other languages. Read Acts 2:14 to find out what Peter did next. He ....

Peter was no longer afraid to tell anyone He knew Jesus. He was glad to tell the good news of Jesus. Read Acts 2:41. How many people were baptized that day to show they believed in Jesus?

2,000   3,000   4,000

Thousands of people joined the disciples and others in believing and trusting in Jesus. How had Peter's choices changed from the time he denied Jesus?

....

What are some things you want to talk to God about in prayer? ....

....

DAY 5

READ EPHESIANS 4:32

In this verse, Paul mentioned three words about how Christians should act. Fill in the blanks:
Be .... and .... to one another, ... one another, just as God also forgave you in Christ.
What are some kind actions you have done today? ....

....

Who are some people you could be kind, caring, and forgiving to in your home? ....

....

What about at school? ....

....

Talk to God about what you want to do. Ask His help to be kind, caring, and forgiving. ....

....

What is God teaching you about Himself this week? What have you learned about yourself? Is there anything you need to spend time praying to God about?

Use this journal page to write out your prayers and any thoughts you have about what God is teaching you this week. Thank Him for teaching you through His Word.

Walking in the Spirit

FRUIT OF THE SPIRIT—
the results of the Holy Spirit's workings in the lives of believers

When a person is guided by the Holy Spirit, the results are peace, love, joy, patience, kindness, goodness, faithfulness, gentleness, and self-control.

KNOW

The Holy Spirit guides us as we live for God's glory.

UNDERSTAND

The Holy Spirit convicts people of sin and helps them make God-honoring choices.

DISCOVER

The Holy Spirit changes the way we think and act to be more like Jesus.

KEY VERSE: "IN WHICH YOU PREVIOUSLY LIVED ACCORDING TO THE WAYS OF THIS WORLD, ACCORDING TO THE RULER OF THE POWER OF THE AIR, THE SPIRIT NOW WORKING IN THE DISOBEDIENT. WE TOO ALL PREVIOUSLY LIVED AMONG THEM IN OUR FLESHLY DESIRES, CARRYING OUT THE INCLINATIONS OF OUR FLESH AND THOUGHTS, AND WE WERE BY NATURE CHILDREN UNDER WRATH AS THE OTHERS WERE ALSO." –EPHESIANS 2:2–3

THE FRUIT OF THE SPIRIT

Paul wrote a letter to the Christians in Galatia. Galatia was a province in Rome, and many of the Christians there were Gentiles, or non-Jews. Paul explained that God changes people who trust in Jesus. God gives them the Holy Spirit, who guides them and gives them power to become more like Jesus. Paul wrote that the Holy Spirit changes the way we think and act. He wanted believers to know that if you let the Holy Spirit guide you, you will do what God wants instead of what you want.

When sin is in control, we do wrong things. We show hatred, jealousy, anger, selfishness, and greed. We fight and get into trouble. People who live like this will not enter God's kingdom. But Jesus frees us from the power of sin. His Holy Spirit lives in us and gives us power to do what is right.

When the Holy Spirit is in control, people choose love, joy, peace, patience, kindness, goodness, faithfulness, gentleness, and self-control. These actions are the fruit of the Spirit—proof that the Spirit is in someone—like how a healthy tree produces fruit. This fruit pleases God. Paul wrote that when we trust in Jesus, we no longer want to do whatever pleases ourselves. The Holy Spirit gives us power to say no to things like hatred, jealousy, anger, selfishness, and greed. The more we know Jesus, the more we will choose actions like joy, kindness, and self-control. We will want to live to please God. Since the Holy Spirit lives in us, we must let the Holy Spirit guide us.

— *based on Galatians 5*

WALKING IN THE SPIRIT

THE WORK OF THE HOLY SPIRIT

The Holy Spirit has at least three ways of helping Christians. Find each one by writing the first letter of the picture in the blank above the picture.
Then read the sentences you created.

THE HOLY SPIRIT

US AS WE LIVE FOR GOD'S GLORY.

THE HOLY SPIRIT

THE WAY WE THINK AND ACT TO BE MORE LIKE JESUS.

THE HOLY SPIRIT

OUR SIN AND HELPS US MAKE CHOICES THAT BRING GOD GLORY.

 DIGGING DEEPER

Read Ephesians 5:15-21. In the wedges, draw or write good things you read that are good for Christians to do.

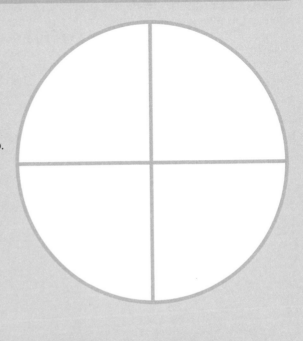

A-MAZING KEY VERSES

Find your way through the maze to the loop at the bottom. Find a path of yellow circles that creates the verse you've been learning. Avoid orange circles as you go! Stop and read each yellow sign as you come to it.

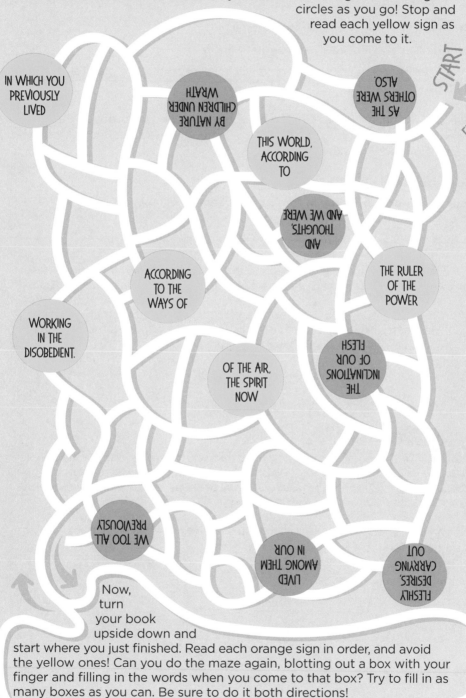

START

EPHESIANS 2:2-3

IN WHICH YOU PREVIOUSLY LIVED

BY NATURE CHILDREN UNDER WRATH

AS THE OTHERS WERE ALSO.

THIS WORLD, ACCORDING TO

AND THOUGHTS, AND WE WERE

ACCORDING TO THE WAYS OF

THE RULER OF THE POWER

WORKING IN THE DISOBEDIENT.

OF THE AIR, THE SPIRIT NOW

THE INCLINATIONS OF OUR FLESH

WE TOO ALL PREVIOUSLY

LIVED AMONG THEM IN OUR

FLESHLY DESIRES, CARRYING OUT

Now, turn your book upside down and start where you just finished. Read each orange sign in order, and avoid the yellow ones! Can you do the maze again, blotting out a box with your finger and filling in the words when you come to that box? Try to fill in as many boxes as you can. Be sure to do it both directions!

WALKING IN THE SPIRIT

DIGGING DAILY

Digging in the Bible means...

➤ reading Bible verses,

➤ thinking about what the verses mean,

➤ discovering what God wants you to know.

At the end of each week's study, you will have a page to use privately as you talk to God in prayer.

Each day will have a Bible passage for you to read and think about. Each day will also have space for you to journal your thoughts, feelings, and questions to God. Now, get digging!

READ GALATIANS 5:1

Paul talked about freedom in this verse. What do you think he meant believers are free from? Choose one of these words:

INSECTS   SIN   WORK

Paul wanted Christians to know they are free from the slavery of sin. Since Jesus takes away our sin, Christians are to live free from the blame and shame of sin.

When you pray today, think about being free from the punishment of sin. Thank Jesus that He has taken that punishment and offered a new identity as child of God for everyone who trusts in Him. ....

....

....

READ GALATIANS 5:7

Paul was not talking about running for exercise. He was talking about people following Jesus. Some of the people had been doing what God wanted. Then others encouraged them to believe lies about Jesus. Those lies made people do bad things. Paul wanted them to change.

Who have you learned will help Christians change the way they think and act to be more like Jesus? ....

....

....

....

Need a hint: The initials are H.S.

Ask God to help you recognize when you hear lies about Him and what He wants you to do. Ask Him to help you live for His glory.

DAY 3

READ EPHESIANS 5:1

Parents help their kids learn to talk by talking to them. As the child grows, he imitates his parents. He learns to talk!

Paul wanted people to imitate God like a child imitates a parent. How could you be an imitator of God? Need help? Read 1 John 4:8 and Psalm 86:5 for clues.

Talk to God about imitating Him. Think of Bible verses about what God is like. Ask God how you can be more like Him.

DAY 4

READ EPHESIANS 5:15

How does this verse tell people to live? ....

....

Read this message in a mirror to find part of what being wise means.

HAVING GOOD SENSE AND JUDGMENT

What is the difference between being wise and being smart? ....

....

What do you want to talk to God about in prayer concerning being wise?

....

....

....

DAY 5

READ EPHESIANS 5:29

Unscramble this word to find out what Christians are to give thanks for.

RYEVEGINTH

Are you supposed to give thanks for having math tests or going to the dentist? ....

A big reason to thank God for everything is to remember that He is in control and He wants good for you. He wants you to learn your math and to have healthy teeth!

Talk to God about things that seem hard to be thankful for. Then thank Him for all the wonderful things you have. You can make notes here if you want. ....

....

....

....

DEFINED

What is God teaching you about Himself this week? What have you learned about yourself? Is there anything you need to spend time praying to God about?

Use this journal page to write out your prayers and any thoughts you have about what God is teaching you this week. Thank Him for teaching you through His Word.

Living on Mission

MISSION—
An assigned task

Jesus told His followers to make disciples of other people. He also promised to be with them to the end of the age as they worked on their mission.

KNOW

God has given us everything we need to live on mission with Him.

UNDERSTAND

We have a real enemy who wants to discourage us from fulfilling our mission.

DISCOVER

Our mission is to make disciples of all nations by the power of the Holy Spirit.

JESUS GAVE THE GREAT COMMISSION

After Jesus had been raised from the dead, He met with His disciples over the next 40 days. During that time, Jesus told them even more about God's kingdom. Then Jesus' eleven disciples went to a mountain in Galilee.

When the disciples saw Jesus, some of them worshiped Him. But some of the disciples still doubted. Then Jesus went up to them and said, "All authority has been given to Me in heaven and on earth." Jesus is God the Son; He always has authority. But after Jesus died on the cross and rose from the dead, God gave Him all authority in heaven and on earth. Jesus is the King over all creation, and He rules over God's kingdom.

Jesus gave the disciples—and everyone who follows Him—a job to do. He said, "Go into all the world and preach the gospel. Make disciples of people from every nation." A disciple is a follower. Jesus wants His followers to tell people all over the world how to be rescued from sin and death by trusting in Jesus' death and resurrection. Then those people who believe would become disciples of Jesus too.

Jesus also said, "Baptize them in the name of the Father and of the Son and of the Holy Spirit." When believers are baptized, they show the world that they have turned from sin and trusted in Jesus as their Savior. Jesus continued, "Teach them to obey everything I have commanded you." Disciples who love Jesus will want to obey Him. Then Jesus said, "Remember this: I am always with you, until the very end of the age."

Jesus also said, "You will receive power when the Holy Spirit has come on you. You will be My witnesses in Jerusalem, in all Judea and Samaria, and to the ends of the earth."

After Jesus said these things, He went up into heaven. The disciples watched Jesus until a cloud hid Him from their sight. All of the sudden, two men appeared. The men were wearing white clothes. These men asked the disciples, "Men of Galilee, why do you stand looking up into heaven? This Jesus, who has been taken from you into heaven, will come again. He will return in the same way that you have seen Him going into heaven."

— based on Matthew 28:16-20 and Acts 1:4-14

DOUBLE MATCH

1. Match each picture of a piece of armor to its title in Ephesians 6:10-20.
2. Number the titles in the same order as in Ephesians 6:10-20.
3. Find the letter in the picture that matches #1. Write the letter in the blank at the bottom of the page. Continue with #2 and so on to #6.
4. Read your message!

1 BELT OF TRUTH

☐ OF THE SPIRIT

RIGHTEOUSNESS LIKE AN ARMOR ON YOUR # ☐

☐ OF FAITH

☐ OF SALVATION

☐ READY FOR GOING

THIS IS WHAT GOD GIVES CHRISTIANS TO HELP THEM FIGHT THE ENEMY.

A ☐ ☐ ☐ ☐ ☐ F ☐ ☐ D
1   2   3   4   5   4   6   4

🔎 DIGGING DEEPER

Did you know that some of the armor of God was mentioned in the Old Testament, long before Paul wrote to the Ephesians? Find Isaiah 59:17. Which words sound like Ephesians 6:15-17?

The verse in Isaiah describes God putting on these special pieces of armor while the verse in Ephesians describes Christians. Think about the word righteousness. It means "right living." What do you think right living is?

How could right living help protect a Christian?

MARK IT UP

During this study, you have worked to memorize Ephesians 2:1-10. You will find the words printed below. Beneath them are instructions for you to mark different things in the Bible passage. You might want to complete each one with a different color pencil, pen, or marker.

Ephesians 2:1-10

(1) And you were dead in your trespasses and sins

(2) in which you previously lived according to the ways of this world, according to the ruler of the power of the air, the spirit now working in the disobedient.

(3) We too all previously lived among them in our fleshly desires, carrying out the inclinations of our flesh and thoughts, and we were by nature children under wrath as the others were also.

(4) But, God, who is rich in mercy, because of his great love that he had for us,

(5) made us alive with Christ even though we were dead in trespasses. You are saved by grace!

(6) He also raised us up with him and seated us with him in the heavens in Christ Jesus,

(7) so that in the coming ages he might display the immeasurable riches of his grace through his kindness to us in Christ Jesus.

(8) For you are saved by grace through faith, and this is not from yourselves; it is God's gift—

(9) not from works, so that no one can boast.

(10) For we are his workmanship, created in Christ Jesus for good works, which God prepared ahead of time for us to do.

Mark the verses above as directed in each of the next steps.

✔ MAKE A CHECK MARK BESIDE THE WORDS JESUS, CHRIST, OR JESUS CHRIST EACH TIME YOU SEE THEM.

" " MAKE QUOTATION MARKS AROUND THE VERSE YOU LIKE BEST IN THIS PASSAGE.

↰ MAKE AN ARROW BESIDE THE VERSE THAT IS HARDEST FOR YOU TO REMEMBER.

☺ MAKE A SMILEY FACE BESIDE THE VERSE THAT IS EASIEST TO REMEMBER.

✺ MAKE A STAR BURST AROUND THE WORD IN VERSE 8 THAT MEANS A PRESENT.

= DOUBLE UNDERLINE IN VERSE 10 WHAT IT SAYS WE ARE.

DIGGING DAILY

Digging in the Bible means...

➤ reading Bible verses,

➤ thinking about what the verses mean,

➤ discovering what God wants you to know.

At the end of each week's study, you will have a page to use privately as you talk to God in prayer.

Each day will have a Bible passage for you to read and think about. Each day will also have space for you to journal your thoughts, feelings, and questions to God. Now, get digging!

READ EPHESIANS 6:11

What reason did Paul give for needing to put on the full armor of God? Circle your answer.

TO PRAY BETTER

TO STAND FIRM AGAINST THE ENEMY

TO TELL MORE PEOPLE ABOUT JESUS

Paul knew that Satan is real and that he lies to people trying to keep them from doing what God wants. God gives the pieces of spiritual armor to help people resist the enemy.

Write your thoughts here, then talk to God about times you need help to know what is true and what is a lie.

READ EPHESIANS 6:14-15

Write the three pieces of God's armor that are listed in these verses.

1)

2)

3)

Truth, righteousness, and readiness (or words like them) tell more about each of the three pieces of armor. Write the correct word next to each piece of armor you listed.

Which of these three pieces of armor do you need most? Talk to God about the help you need and thank Him for hearing your prayer. Write your other thoughts here.

DAY **3**

READ EPHESIANS 6:16

Why do people need the shield of faith?

Flaming darts are the lies and temptations the enemy uses to try and tempt people away from God. Different people are tempted to do wrong by different things.

When might you be tempted to do something wrong?

Faith is trust and belief. When you are tempted to do wrong, your trust and belief in Jesus can help you make the right choice.

Remember, you can always talk to God. He knows what tempts you. He knows how hard it is to stay away from doing wrong. Tell God how you are feeling.

DAY 4

READ EPHESIANS 6:17

If you looked up today's Bible verse, you used the sword of the Spirit! God's Word can always guide you in the right path.

Do you have a favorite Bible verse? Write it here or write where it is in the Bible.

Did you know you can pray Bible verses? You might want to pray one of these today:

PSALM 117:1–2   PSALM 119:16   PSALM 126:3

DAY 5

READ EPHESIANS 6:18

Doesn't it feel great to know you can pray about anything? God always wants to hear from you. You can tell Him what makes you feel good, what makes you feel bad, or scared, or worried, or lonely, or anything else you can think of!

How are you feeling today? Talk to God about what makes you happy, sad, scared, worried, or anything else.

You can make notes about these verses or your prayer here.

What is God teaching you about Himself this week? What have you learned about yourself? Is there anything you need to spend time praying to God about?

Use this journal page to write out your prayers and any thoughts you have about what God is teaching you this week. Thank Him for teaching you through His Word.

Parent Guide

Created by God

God made people in His image and for His glory. As the Creator, God determines the purpose of His creation. He has the authority to define what is true about His creation—including people. Your identity is who God says you are.

Key Verse: Ephesians 2:10
Key Passage: God Created People (Genesis 1–2)

BIBLE STORY

Together read the Bible story on page 7 of your child's Activity Book and ask the following review questions.

> **Q1:** What day of creation did God make people?
> **A1:** On the 6th day *(Gen. 1:26-27, 31)*
> **Q2:** How did God create Adam?
> **A2:** He formed Adam from the dust and breathed life into him. *(Gen. 2:7)*
> **Q3:** How did God create Eve?
> **A3:** God put Adam into a deep sleep. He took one of his ribs and made a woman. *(Gen. 2: 21-22)*
> **Q4:** How did God make people?
> **A4:** God made people in His image and for His glory. *(Gen. 1:27, Col. 1:16)*

DEEPER STUDY

Read Ephesians 1 together and discuss the questions.

> **Q1:** When did God plan for people?
> **A1:** Before He created the world *(Eph 1:4)*
> **Q2:** What can Jesus provide for a person?

> **A1:** Redemption and forgiveness from sin according to His grace *(Eph 1:7)*
> **Q3:** What did God put Jesus above?
> **A3:** Everything *(Eph 1:20-22)*
> **Q4:** Who has the authority to determine your identity?
> **A4:** God
> **Q5:** What does it mean to be created in God's image?
> **A5:** When we say God created us in His image, it means we have many similar qualities to God. He gave us these qualities so that we can glorify Him in unique ways.

PRAY AND JOURNAL

Thank God for planning for you before He created the world. Praise Him for creating you uniquely in His image. Ask Him to help you as you live for His glory.

Encourage your child to complete the daily Bible study and journal pages in the activity book this week.

Broken by Sin

This week focuses on our identity broken by sin. God created all people in His image and for His glory, but we have sinned and rebelled against God. Sin separates us from God, but God still loves us. God promised a Rescuer would come from Eve's family. God sent His Son, Jesus, to rescue people from sin and bring them back to God.

Key Verse: Ephesians 2:1
Key Passage: Sin Entered the World (Genesis 3)

BIBLE STORY

Together read the Bible story on page 15 of your child's Activity Book and ask the following review questions.

> **Q1:** What did the serpent first say to Eve?
> **A1:** "Did God really say, 'You can't eat from any tree in the garden?'" *(Gen. 3:1)*
> **Q2:** What did the serpent say would happen if Eve ate the fruit?
> **A2:** She would not die. She would be like God, knowing good and evil. *(Gen. 3:5)*
> **Q3:** What happened after Adam and Eve ate the fruit?
> **A3:** They realized what they had done. They tried to cover themselves and hide from God. *(Gen. 3:7-8)*

DEEPER STUDY

Read Ephesians 2:1-5 together and discuss the following questions.

> **Q1:** What does it mean to sin?
> **A1:** To sin is to think, say, or behave in any way that goes against God and His commands

> **A1:** Why do you think Adam and Eve sinned?
> **A1:** Adam and Eve did not trust God's plan and they disobeyed God.
> **Q2:** What do these verses tell us about our sin?
> **A2:** Because of our sins, we are separated from God and our identity is broken.
> **Q3:** Read Eph. 2:4-5. What hope do these verses give us about our identity?
> **A3:** God is merciful and loves us. He sent Jesus for us to be forgiven of our sin when we trust in Him.

PRAY AND JOURNAL

Pray together, thanking God for showing you through His Word what is true about all people because of sin. Thank Him for sending Jesus to rescue us from sin when we trust in Him.

Encourage your child to complete the daily Bible study and journal pages in the activity book this week.

Transformed by the Gospel

When we trust in Jesus, we aren't just saying that we agree with the idea of Jesus as God's Son. Through the gospel, God opens our eyes to who Jesus really is. We put our trust in Him, believing that His death on the cross provides forgiveness for our sins and that because He was raised from the dead, He is King over everything. When we trust in Jesus, He changes our hearts. He removes our identity of sin and gives us a new identity—child of God!

Key Verse: Ephesians 2:8-9
Key Passage: Saul's Conversion (Acts 8–9)

BIBLE STORY

Together read the Bible story on page 23 of your child's Activity Book and ask the following review questions.
> **Q1:** What did Saul intend to do in Damascus?
> **A1:** Arrest Christians *(Acts 9:2)*
> **Q2:** What happened to Saul on the way to Damascus?
> **A2:** A light blinded him, and Jesus spoke to him. *(Acts 9:3-6)*
> **Q3:** God told Ananias He had a plan for Saul. What was God's plan?
> **A3:** To tell the Gentiles about Jesus *(Acts 9:15)*
> **Q4:** What did Saul begin to do after he could see again?
> **A4:** To speak in the synagogues about Jesus *(Acts 9:20)*

DEEPER STUDY

Read Ephesians 2:1-10 together and discuss the following questions.
> **Q1:** This passage teaches us about sin. What does it mean that we sinned against God?
> **A1:** God cannot be around sin.

Sin separates us from God and deserves God's punishment of death. *(Eph. 2:1-3; Romans 6:23)*
> **Q2:** What did God provide for us?
> **A2:** God provided His Son Jesus to rescue us from the punishment we deserve. *(Eph. 2: 4-5)*
> **Q3:** What is God's salvation?
> **A3:** God's salvation is a gift that every person needs and can receive. *(Eph 2:8-9)*
> **Q4:** What happens when a person trusts in Jesus for salvation?
> **A4:** When someone trusts in Jesus as Savior, her whole identity is transformed!

PRAY AND JOURNAL

Pray with your child, thanking God for sending Jesus. Praise Him for rescuing people who are dead in their sin and making them alive.

Encourage your child to complete the daily pages in the activity book this week. Be available to answer any questions about the gospel or trusting in Jesus for salvation.

Who We Are in Christ

God defines the true identity of all followers of Jesus. When we trust in Jesus for salvation, our identity is changed and transformed by the gospel. Like fruit grows when it is connected to the vine, Christians grow to look more like Jesus when we are connected to Him. Jesus rescues us from sin and frees us to live a life that honors God. By doing what is good and right, people who trust Jesus can show that they really believe in Him.

Key Verse: Ephesians 2:4-5
Key Passage: The Vine and the Branches (John 15:1-8)

BIBLE STORY

Together read the Bible story on page 31 of your child's Activity Book and ask the following review questions.

> **Q1:** Who is the true vine and gardener in this story?
> **A1:** Jesus is the true vine and God the Father is the gardener *(John 15:1)*
> **Q2:** Who does Jesus say are the branches?
> **A2:** The branches are people who trust in Jesus. *(John 15:5)*
> **Q3:** How did the branches produce fruit in Jesus' parable?
> **A3:** The branches stayed connected to Jesus to produce fruit. *(John 15:4-5)*

Comment that Jesus told this parable or story about the vine and branches to help His disciples understand that they are now transformed, or changed because they trust in Jesus. Jesus referred to their hearts changing—their identity.

DEEPER STUDY

Read Ephesians 2:1-5 together and discuss the following questions.

> **Q1:** What does God teach you through these verses?
> **A1:** All people sin against God and are separated from Him, but God provided Jesus so we can be saved through grace
> **Q2:** What does the word adopted mean?
> **A2:** Adoption is when God welcomes us into His family as His children.
> **Q3:** How can Christians grow to look more like Jesus?
> **A3:** By obeying God's Word, saying no to sin with the help of the Holy Spirit, and loving others like Jesus loves Christians can show others we really believe in Jesus.

PRAY AND JOURNAL

Pray together, asking God for His help to abide in Him, say no to sin, and love others like Jesus loves.

Encourage your child to complete the daily pages in the activity book this week. Be available to answer any questions throughout the week.

What We Have in Christ

Jesus came to seek and save the lost. Explain that people sometimes use the word lost to describe people whose identity is broken by sin and without God, those who have not trusted Jesus as their Savior. Jesus taught people that He came to save people from their sins. Just like people are happy when something lost is found, all of heaven is happy when a person turns from sin to trusting in Jesus.

Key Verse: Ephesians 2:5-6
Key Passage: Jesus Taught Three Parables

BIBLE STORY

Together read the Bible story on page 39 of your child's Activity Book and ask the following review questions.

> **Q1:** Jesus spent time teaching people whom the religious leaders did not like. Who were they?
> **A1:** Sinners and tax collectors *(Luke 15:2)*
> **Q2:** What did that man do when he found his lost sheep?
> **A2:** He invited his friends and neighbors to celebrate with him. *(Luke 15:6)*
> **Q3:** What did the woman do when she lost one of her coins?
> **A3:** She lit a lamp and searched the house carefully until she found it. *(Luke 15:8)*
> **Q4:** How did the father greet the younger son in the third parable when he returned home?
> **A5:** He greeted his son warmly, joyfully, lovingly, and with compassion. *(Luke 15:20)*

DEEPER STUDY

Read Ephesians 1:3-8 and 13 together and discuss the following questions.

> **Q1:** Read verses 3-8 and complete the following statements: I am _____; I am _____; I am _____; I am _____; I am _____; I am _____. Discuss the meaning of each of these identities with your child.
> **A1:** I am blessed, I am chosen, I am adopted, I am redeemed, I am forgiven, I am sealed
> **Q2:** Which one of these statements is easiest or more difficult to identify with and believe? Explain.
> **A2:** Answers will vary.

PRAY AND JOURNAL

Pray with your child, thanking God for all of the spiritual blessings He gives us in Jesus when we trust in Him. Ask Him to help you family remember your identity this week— who God says you are.

Encourage your child to complete the daily Bible study and journal pages in eek. Be available to answer any questions throughout the week.

Living Out Our Identity

Some people think the Bible is mostly just rules about what to do and what not to do. While there certainly are instructions about how to live, the Bible is not just a list of rules God wants us to follow. The gospel transforms us from the inside out. Our minds and hearts change to understand God better and love Him more, and then our behavior changes because of our new thoughts and new desires.

Key Verse: Ephesians 2:2-3
Key Passage: Peter Denied Jesus and Was Forgiven (Luke 22:31-34; 54-62; John 21:1-19; Acts 2)

BIBLE STORY

Together read the Bible story on page 47 of your child's Activity Book and ask the following review questions.

> **Q1:** What did Peter do three times before the rooster crowed?
> **A1:** Peter denied Jesus. *(Luke 22:54-60)*
> **Q2:** When Peter realized that he had denied Jesus, what did he do?
> **A2:** Peter went outside and wept bitterly. *(Luke 22:62)*
> **Q3:** What question did Jesus ask Peter three times?
> **A3:** "Peter, do you love me?" *(John 21:15, 16, 17)*
> **Q4:** How did Peter answer Jesus' questions?
> **A4:** "Yes, Lord. You know I love You." *(John 21:15, 16, 17)*
> **Q5:** What did Peter do when people heard the disciples speaking in many languages?
> **A5:** He stood up and preached to the people, telling them that Jesus was the Messiah. *(Acts 2:14)*

DEEPER STUDY

Read Ephesians 4:22-24 together and discuss the following questions.

> **Q1:** What did Paul mean when He talked about the "old self"?
> **A1:** Paul meant that Christians have a new identity in Jesus.
> **Q2:** What does it mean to put on the "new self"?
> **A2:** Putting on the "new self" means choosing actions that look more like Jesus. Our minds and hearts change to understand God better and love Him more, and then our behavior changes because of our new thoughts and new desires.
> **Q3:** What does verse 24 teach us about this "new self"?
> **A3:** The "new self" was created according to God's likeness in righteousness and purity of truth.

PRAY AND JOURNAL

Pray together, thanking God for teaching your child what it looks like to live out the Christian life. Praise God for always forgiving us of our sin and sending the Holy Spirit to help guide us as we live for God's glory.

Walking in the Spirit

When we trust in Jesus, the Holy Spirit begins to change us. Paul told the believers in the Galatian church how to recognize that God is working in someone's life. People who are saved by Jesus become more like Him, and the Holy Spirit gives them power to say no to sin and to live in a way that pleases God.

Key Verse: Ephesians 2:2-3
Key Passage: The Fruit of the Spirit (Galatians 5)

BIBLE STORY

Read the Bible story for Session 7 on page 55 of your child's Activity Book and ask the following review questions.

> **Q1:** Who did Paul write this letter to?
> **A1:** The church at Galatia *(Gal. 1:2)*
> **Q2:** When the Holy Spirit is in control, what actions to people choose?
> **A2:** Love, joy, peace, patience, kindness, goodness, faithfulness, gentleness, and self-control. *(Gal. 5:22-23)*
> **Q3:** What does the fruit of the Spirit mean?
> **A3:** These actions are proof that the Spirit is in someone. The more we know Jesus, the more we choose these actions.

DEEPER STUDY

Mention that the Bible helps us know at least three things about the Holy Spirit: The Holy Spirit comforts us, shows us our sin, and guides us as we live for God's glory. Read the following verses and discuss.

> **Q1:** Read John 16:13 together. Who is the "Spirit of truth"? What did Jesus say He would do when He came?
> **A1:** The "Spirit of truth" is the Holy Spirit. Jesus told His followers that the Holy Spirit would guide them.
> **Q2:** Read John 16:8 together. What else does the Holy Spirit do?
> **A2:** The Holy Spirit shows us our sin.
> **Q3:** Read Ephesians 5:15 together. What does this verse instruct believers to do?
> **A3:** This verse tells believers to live wisely. Believers can live wisely by praying to God, reading and obeying the Bible, trusting in God's promises, and growing to look more like Jesus.

PRAY AND JOURNAL

Pray together, thanking God for His Word to teach your family more about the Holy Spirit. Ask the Holy Spirit to comfort you, show you sin in your life, and guide your family as you live for God's glory.

Encourage your child to complete the daily pages this week.

Living on Mission

Jesus gave the disciples the Great Commission, but it wasn't just for them. It is a command for all of us. Every person who believes in Jesus has a responsibility to share the gospel—the good news about Jesus. Our mission is to make disciples of all nations by the power of the Holy Spirit.

Key Verse: Ephesians 2:10
Key Passage: Jesus Gave the Great Commission (Matthew 28:16-20; Acts 1:4-14)

BIBLE STORY

Read the Bible story for Session 8 on page 63 of your child's Activity Book and ask the following review questions.

> **Q1:** What had been given to Jesus in heaven and on earth?
> **A1:** All authority *(Matt. 28:18)*
> **Q2:** What was the job Jesus had for His disciples?
> **A2:** Go make disciples of all nations, baptizing them in the name of the Father, the Son, and the Holy Spirit, teaching them to observe everything He has commanded them. *(Matt. 28:19)*
> **Q3:** What was the last thing Jesus told them?
> **A3:** He would be with them. *(Matt. 28:20)*
> **Q4:** What is our mission?
> **A4:** Our mission as believers is to make disciples of all nations by the power of the Holy Spirit.

DEEPER STUDY

Read Ephesians 6:10-20 together. Remind your child that the armor of God is not a physical armor that we carry around or wear. The armor Paul talks about was his way of communicating the protection God gives believers to live on mission. Discuss the following questions.

> **Q1:** How does learning about the armor of God encourage us?
> **A1:** Learning about the armor of God reminds us that God has given us everything we need to live on mission for Him.
> **Q2:** Who is our battle against?
> **A2:** Our battle is against Satan and the powers of evil.
> **Q3:** Besides putting on the armor of God, what did Paul tell the church to do?
> **A3:** He told the church to pray at all times in the Spirit.

PRAY AND JOURNAL

Lead your child in prayer, thanking God for giving us what we need to live on mission and stand strong against evil. Pray that God would guide your family to fight the good fight and expand His kingdom.

Encourage your child to complete the daily pages in the activity book this week. Look back with your child and discuss what God has taught him through this study.

CERTIFICATE OF COMPLETION

THIS CERTIFICATE IS AWARDED TO

ON

DATE

FOR COMPLETING

DEFINED

WHO GOD SAYS YOU ARE

PARENT OR LEADER'S SIGNATURE